5/67 Problem Solving

by

Craig Humphreys &

Dr. Len Bertain

Humphreys & Bertain

Additional copies of this book may be obtained

from your local bookstore or the publisher:

CEO University Press

3758 Grand Avenue, Suite 25

Oakland, CA 94610

510-520-8011

For more information on the concepts and processes described in this book please contact:

The War on Waste Academy

Las Vegas, NV

Tel: (510) 520-8011

len@solvewickedproblems.guru

craig@solvewickedproblems.guru

5/67 Problem Solving: How to Solve Wicked Problems Correctly © 2017

By: Craig Humphreys & Leonard Bertain

Copyright War on Waste training materials 1993-2017

No Blame is a registered trademark of The War on Waste Academy

All rights reserved.

Except for the usual review purposes, no part of this work may be reproduced or transmitted in any form or by any means, electronic or mechanical, including photocopy, or any information retrieval system, without the permission of the publisher.

Manufactured in the United States of America

ISBN-13: 978-1976400803

ISBN-10: 1976400805

5/67 Problem Solving

How to Solve Wicked Problems...correctly

Craig Humphreys

Len Bertain, PhD

War on Waste Academy

Las Vegas, NV

Humphreys & Bertain

Table of Contents

Introduction

1. What is 5/67 Problem Solving?
2. The 5/67 Ah Ha! Moment
3. How to Solve Incredibly Difficult Problems
4. 5/67 Tools: The Yes/No Chart
5. 5/67 Tools: $50 / $500 / $5000 Task Log
6. 5/67 Speed Analysis
7. 5/67 Projects: Starting is Better than Being Right
8. Good Enough Is - The 5/67 Mantra
9. Perfection is the Enemy of Good
10. How to Solve Wicked Problems
11. 95/33 Thinking: Your Government At Work
12. The No Blame Game: Change without Reprisal
13. Pioneers & Settlers: Blending The Perfect Team
14. 5/67 Thinking is a Non-linear process
15. 5/67 Take Aways: Better Projects, Better Decisions

INTRODUCTION

We have decided to write this book as a result of lessons learned from our collective 60 years of consulting experience. In that time we have participated in solving over 10,000 problems and leading those projects to completion. While doing so we have repeatedly seen leaders and executives sponsoring and supporting inefficient approaches to completing complex projects and initiatives, almost always to their career and business detriment. We have successfully been teaching 5/67 Thinking as a way to improve the quality of decision-making and project execution in our clients' businesses. This book is our way to share these very successful techniques with current and future business leaders, managers, executives so they, too, can solve difficult and even Wicked Problems.

First off, we offer a discussion of the three classes of problems as we see them. They are: stupid problems, difficult problems, and Wicked Problems. We like to capitalize the words Wicked Problems because of the unique and challenging nature of that type of problem.

The characteristics of the three problem types are summarized below, and covered in great detail in subsequent chapters:

- **Stupid problems**: These are problems for which a ready and simple solution exists. Rarely is extensive measurement and analysis required, but rather a 5/67 Thinking mindset is sufficient to solve such problems. An example of this problem occurred at a law office when the Managing Partner ignored the plea by the secretaries that they were backlogged at the single printer that they shared. By simply adding a few printers the secretaries and paralegals didn't have to wait for their documents, which increased the output of the lawyers and thus the profitability of the law firm by over $2 million annually. That was a stupid problem.

- **Difficult problems**: These are problems that are simply not easy to solve. Most every project team has insufficient expertise, insight, and knowledge to fully solve a difficult problem at the outset. Difficult problems are best solved through decomposition and an incremental, 5/67 Thinking approach wherein project team members learn, gain insights, and develop new approaches through the successive iterations of problem solving. The NASA initiative to put a man on the moon by the end of 1969 is an example of how to properly solve a difficult problem through incremental problem solving after decomposing the problem into manageable, independent phases.

- **Wicked Problems**: These are the pinnacle of problems to tackle. Wicked Problems simply are not susceptible to ordinary problem solving techniques and, more than likely, the problem solvers have never dealt with such a problem before. Further, Wicked Problems are exemplified by one particularly unpleasant attribute - most approaches to tackling the problem simply make the problem worse. Long-standing corporate inefficiencies, government policies towards welfare, foreign policy, and healthcare, the War on Drugs, homelessness, and many other problems all fall into this category. Solving these problems demands accepting that we don't know enough to solve the entire problem straight away. So commencing with careful measurement and analysis is required to avoid making the problem worse. A minimum resource expenditure with an iterative approach to making progress is the only way to achieve success. We regard the Werner von Braun rocket development team after World War II as an example of how to properly solve a Wicked Problem. That team did intense analysis, developed tests, failed, learned, and repeated. They started off with well documented, unpleasant failures, but ultimately succeeded in developing very reliable lift systems that took Mercury, Gemini, and Apollo missions into space. And, they managed to avoid many of the awful side effects of a poor approach to a Wicked Problem such as killing themselves, creating really bad publicity, losing their funding, and so forth.

As you read the following chapters, remember that *5/67 Problem Solving: How to Solve Wicked Problems...Correctly* is all about bringing clarity to the process of problem solving, particularly difficult and Wicked Problems. Throughout their careers the authors have focused on the ROI and the waste elimination aspects of the problems that they encountered. In all cases, difficult and Wicked problems have been a challenge, even for us. But by sticking to the basics of the concepts that we are laying out in this book, we have been extremely successful working through the challenges provided by these problems. Somewhat to our surprise, we have learned over and over that it is OK to be wrong and that is a key message that we want to leave with our readers.

> **...we have learned over and over that it is OK to be wrong...**

In addition, we offer "No Blame" as a mandatory protection mantra for "Problem Solving Change without reprisal." When solutions don't work or a solution improves our understanding of the problem, we get excited because on one hand, we have advanced progress on the solution and in the other, we know another way that didn't work. And if a No Blame culture is present, great progress and profitable change can happen, as no one involved fears reprisal for the original bad solution.

Enjoy the read. The authors hope that after you are done you will feel more comfortable tackling those difficult problems and Wicked Problems when you encounter them.

CHAPTER 1

What is 5/67 Problem Solving?

5/67 Problem Solving is an approach we will extensively teach in this book wherein problems are first characterized and then a mindset adopted which permits solving problems in the most efficient way possible. The techniques we present in this book are the result of the authors combined consulting and problem solving work over many decades. They have been tried, tested, and proven in a wide variety of situations, from the Fortune 100 to small businesses, from government to military. 5/67 Problem Solving works everywhere.

So, why the name "5/67 Problem Solving"? This is based on the statistically valid premise that, if applied correctly, 5% of all available resources can yield as much as 67% of all possible benefits. Think about that for a moment. Wouldn't it be great to always get two thirds of your project objective and only spend 5% of your budget? At this point in our presentations of 5/67 Problem Solving we are usually facing an audience that is composed entirely of skeptical and incredulous people. This is because we have all faced problems. We have all tried to tackle problems of various levels of difficulty, and, in many cases, we haven't all done very well. Wouldn't it be nice to say after dealing successfully with a particularly difficult problem: "heck, I still have 95% of my budget available to solve another 19 problems!".

Thus the incredulity and skepticism.

Often we ask our audiences to suspend their disbelief for a moment (this always gets a chuckle), and we ask them, "Have you ever completed a project and afterwards you and your project team members commented, 'if we had only known that beforehand'?". "Have you ever tackled a difficult problem where everyone assigned to solve the problem had full knowledge of the problem and 100% skills in every available solution technique?"

We call the moment associated with the first question a moment of awareness known as the "Ah Ha!" moment. We refer to the second question as a syllogism. Nobody ever has 100% knowledge of a difficult problem and the techniques to solve it. If they did, we can deduce that the problem would already be gone.

Our second question addresses a fundamental principle of problem solving, known as "incrementalism". It's perfectly OK to expend your 5% of resources to solve part of a problem, especially if the problem is particularly challenging. Even if you don't make as much progress as you hoped, some wonderful things can happen. Your team gets smarter about the problem, new ideas are generated, and a team feels some spirit from having made progress in a working environment where progress is celebrated instead of dealing with an unrealistic demand for "instant results" from management. We'll cover this in great detail later.

Our consulting practice abounds with examples of problems where 5/67 solutions existed, but our clients were on the path of very expensive, inappropriate, or ill-advised solutions. We refer to ill-advised solutions as examples of "95/33" thinking, as in, spending 95% of all of the money available in hopes of garnering some small benefit. We see this all too often when project leaders are under great pressure to "just do something!".

In one such example, we had a client surgery center which was falling further and further behind in scheduling operations. They had determined that $6 million dollars were needed to be spent on a new surgery wing in order to meet the demand. However, when we looked carefully at their operations, we noticed that only 50% of available surgery center time each day was spent performing surgeries. The rest of the time was spent cleaning up after a surgery, or preparing the rooms for the next scheduled surgery. We analyzed the cleanup and preparation process and found multiple inefficiencies. By working with the single cleanup person, we assembled a cleanup and preparation crew. A number of great ideas were developed, all of which helped to reduce the setup and cleanup dramatically. Surgery productivity increased from 50% of the available time to 80%, which is a 60% increase in productivity.

This is an example of 5/67 Thinking. Seeking the simple and efficient way to solve a problem. In this example there were two views of the problem. The surgeons believed their problem was insufficient capacity, so they said, "We need a new wing". Whereas we defined their problem as, "You are using your existing facility inefficiently and you need a cleanup team not a single person."

In another example, we were asked to assess why a technology company was experiencing relatively poor results from their software development and IT operations teams. The presumption by the client management going into the project was that the underlying processes had some fundamental defects and we could fix them. In other words, this relatively enlightened client believed they had a difficult process problem and process experts could help them. A very refreshing situation to tackle! And, totally wrong.

It turns out this client had a very process oriented, regimented, disciplined, and stoic lady in charge of their software development team. They had an inspirational, creative, and somewhat disorganized, but endearing man in charge of their IT operations team. After a two full days of analyzing their process documents, we conducted interviews with the two managers. We went straightaway to the CEO's office and advised him that he didn't have a difficult problem. He had a stupid problem. He merely needed to swap the jobs of the two managers, as the two individually were ideally suited to the other manager's job. After several seconds of silence he looked up and said, "How could I not have seen that before? Of course!"

Why would you wish to continue reading this book and learning what we have to teach? Because being an excellent problem solver is an immensely valuable skill, will create new career opportunities for you, and will generally reduce your problem solving anxiety. You will definitely benefit from having an elevated understanding of how to define, break down and solve all sorts of problems.

That is what we at the War on Waste Academy are offering in this book. If that interests you, please read on!

CHAPTER 2

The 5/67 Ah Ha! Moment

The Ah Ha! moment is usually the moment of awareness when a project manager or team realizes that they could have taken a simple, direct approach to solve a problem as opposed to the approach actually taken. Ideally these moments of realization can happen before a poor project plan is selected and a substantial amount of resources expended on a failed, expensive, or overly complex solution attempt.

We've all been there, however. Sitting around a table doing a post-mortem on a project, project teams sit looking at each other wondering why in the world they didn't think of "that" approach before starting the project. That is what this chapter is about - fostering the environment wherein creative, efficient ideas are put forth to actually find 5/67 approaches before projects are commissioned. That is 5/67 Thinking at work.

It is first useful to address just why these Ah Ha! Moments tend to occur after projects are completed, rather than before the project starts. There are a number of common factors that contribute to suppressing novel ideas and efficient approaches to solving problems and selecting a project approach. First, when executives and managers typically seek solutions to a problem, they typically want a solution to the entire problem. Leaders aren't commonly open to accepting partial solutions or incremental progress when planning a project. So, creative ideas that can lead to improved insight into solving a problem during an iterative solution strategy are discarded or rejected even if a rapid 5% solution might contribute significant profits to the organization (For example, rapid time to market). Second, many organizational cultures are beset with a top-down mentality wherein managers and executives tend to dictate problem solving strategies to their teams (after all, they are the leaders and responsible for strategy, right?). This kind of culture and mentality prevent the solicitation and collection of ideas from the team which will actually implement the project. These organizations are ones in which project execution is prosaic, results are mediocre, and the expectation of remarkable achievement is slowly crushed out of the organization.

From our consulting practice there are some really interesting Ah Ha! Moments that have come up. The common thread in arriving at these Ah Ha! Moments tend to be either doing careful measurements, or actively getting the participation of the employees most closely associated with the problem.

At Fed Ex we were involved in addressing the problem of how to quickly unload the truck at its depot. The truck drivers and crew were under intense time pressure to speed thing up. Our Ah Ha! Moment occurred when the time to unload truck was measured and the unload time was directly tied to how many people could be in truck at any time. This led to the solution. They changed the loading of the large semi trucks from rear end loading to side loading which increased the number of people who could unload, which, in turn, dramatically reduce the unload/load time.

A produce company was planning to build two storage buildings in the area of where their vegetable fields were located at a cost of over $2 Million for the 2 buildings. The Ah Ha! Moment occurred when, during our group discussions, one of employees looked at costs of moving trucks from field with vegetables and figured that if they equipped a semi trailer with all the cleaning and packaging equipment that they could reduce handling and time of moving vegetables from field to distribution center. This employee suddenly realized that the problem wasn't storage, but rather a process inefficiency where cleaning and packaging could only be done after initial transportation from the fields. Eventually this approach became known as "a factory in the field" and set a new standard of performance for the industry.

So, what is the purpose of seeking the Ah Ha! moment? Our clients often have asked this question, as they feel we are chasing an ephemeral objective. Fortunately, there are solid justifications for seeking the Ah Ha! Moment before executing a project to solve a problem. First is awareness at the executive and decision-making level that any organization's typical project plans and problem solutions are rarely the 5/67 approach. They usually reflect the biases and traditions of the organization itself, and are often responses to pressures such as "solve this problem and solve it right now!" Executives that are aware that a 5/67 solution probably exists to their problem will be willing to entertain ideas, make incremental progress, and invest some time and energy to find this optimal solution. This 5/67 mindset always pays substantial dividends to the organization.

Secondly, managers and executives learn to challenge and push their teams to find more innovative and simple solutions to problems. It takes some time to "train" an organization to adjust its thinking in this manner, but if it can, the benefit is huge. The time requirement exists because changing a company's culture around problem solving does not happen overnight. Whether you call it tradition, killing sacred cows, or corporate inertia, it takes time and energy to convince a group of people to do things differently than they are accustomed. Practical steps that executives can take include allowing and encouraging their teams to learn and make progress on difficult problems rather than attempting to solve them all at once. (See chapters 3 and 11 on difficult problems and 95/33 thinking). Executives can also encourage ideas and suggestions, gather groups of employees closest to problems for round-table discussions, and carefully avoid assigning blame to those responsible for old, inefficient processes. In addition, celebrating progress and incremental wins rapidly builds a culture of positivity and support for the teams, which tends to lead to greater participation and energy. It is an impressive positive cycle when done correctly, and a very dismal negative cycle when done wrong.

Finally, we have a technique we've used in our executive roles over the years that has proven itself to be repeatedly effective. It's the "What can you do?" question.

This question arises when an employee, partner, associate, or team member walks into your office and states, "We have X problem and we can't solve it". Or, says words to that effect. Our constant and consistent response has always been, "OK then. What can you do?"

This challenge of "What can you do?" is intended to empower employees, provide them executive support that making incremental progress is perfectly acceptable, and creating a culture where failing to immediately solve a difficult problem is not a career threatening event. Further, teams that are readily able to make incremental progress tend to make better measurements, define project success more clearly, and develop new and innovative ways to attack the problem as they make progress. They become incremental problem solvers, which leads to better results on difficult problems.

Ultimately, this "What can you do?" managerial tool will lead to having team members who think for themselves, challenge themselves, and become 5/67 Thinkers on their own.

CHAPTER 3

How to Solve Difficult Problems

Don't. Most successful problem solvers, including both authors, believe they have never solved a difficult problem in their lives. Instead, they tackle the aspect of the difficult problem they best understand, learn, make progress, and iterate. During each little phase of progress the problem solver becomes smarter about the issue and gains insights into new ways to make progress.

The admonition "Don't solve difficult problems" sounds like trite and glib advice. Yet, we cannot overemphasize the importance of this point. Attempting to "swallow whole" a difficult problem, or even worse, a Wicked Problem, leads to wasteful spending, unpleasant unintended consequences, and often having to deal with a problem that is worse than when you started. In this chapter we endeavor to make our case that attacking a difficult problem or Wicked Problem in its entirety is always a bad strategy.

The world is full of complex and difficult problems. We encounter them in our personal lives, at work, in industry, and in government. These are problems that have often lingered for years, been ignored by prior leaders or managers, or have been made worse by prior attempts to solve them. Some difficult problems are so complex we call them Wicked Problems. We cover Wicked Problems in a later chapter.

As indicated in the introduction, we categorize all problems into three buckets. Stupid, Difficult, and Wicked. Here are some examples of well-known difficult problems:

- Sending a man to the moon was a difficult problem. Notice we categorize this as difficult not Wicked. The reason for this is there was a clear path to the final success, albeit with numerous challenges such as weight, lift system optimization, re-entry heat dissipation, and life-support systems. And, all of these had to fit into the overall guidance system computations, which were not at all easy to perform in 1968 and 1969. There was indeed a lot of work to be done but the individual steps were clear, and there were no major side-effects or unintended consequences associated with the success or failure of intermediate project results. This lack of major side effects and unintended consequences is why putting a man on the moon was a difficult problem, admittedly of grand proportions. In the end, reaching the moon and returning was like solving a really tough physics and engineering problem.

- Unraveling the mystery of DNA structure into its actual double helix structure was also a difficult problem. At the time of this discovery there were competing teams trying to figure out the true structure of DNA. Linus Pauling in the US at Caltech (who initially proposed single strand DNA structure), Maurice Wilkins at Cambridge, Kings College (who was trying to unravel the DNA structure purely from x-ray diffraction patterns), Rosalind Franklin at Cambridge - Kings College (who had a very similar approach as Wilkins), and, the team which first succeeded in publishing the right answer, Watson and Crick at Cambridge, who first tried to explain the DNA structure with a triple strand but then settled on double helix.

The approach these teams took to solving a difficult problem is an excellent case study in proper technique. Each small increment of information about the structure of DNA allowed each of the teams to move their research forward. They all learned and gained insights from information about incremental progress made by themselves and others, where available. Now, since this was a competitive research objective the information sharing was imperfect, which is perhaps the only aspect of difficult problem solving where these teams collectively fell short of ideal. As history shows, Watson and Crick first proposed the double helix structure of DNA, which perfectly fit the available data and precisely explained cell division and x-ray diffraction observations.

- Most problems are not simple, or as we call them, stupid problems.. Economics, education, budgeting, long-standing business problems that have been ignored for an extended period of time, research problems, all of these are examples of difficult problems, some of them are even Wicked Problems. Our approach to solving difficult problems is to break them down into smaller, simpler problems. Most difficult problems can be readily decomposed when examined from the right perspective. This is what we call the 5/67 Thinking perspective where straightforward and ready progress can be made. Obtaining the right perspective on a difficult problem is achieved through repeated measurements and consideration, once a clear and concise definition of a successful outcome is understood by everyone involved.

- We have been frequently asked, "How did you solve so many difficult problems in your careers?" And in fact, viewed from afar, we have both solved extremely difficult technology, engineering, and business problems. Examples of difficult problems that we have ultimately solved include developing an algorithm to increase the OPRA (Option Price Reporting Authority) tick distribution speed by 100x, dramatically increasing the productivity of dozens of factories and businesses, and developing very sophisticated national intelligence data collection systems still in use today. At the outset these problems appeared intractable and had been tackled unsuccessfully by multiple teams prior to our involvement. From our perspective, the past failures were due to improper problem definition, inadequate measurements to gain insights into the problem, and a penchant for seeking a 95/33 "solve it all at once" problem solving approach.

- As stated before, we claim we have never solved a

difficult problem in our lives. Some readers may argue that we are engaging in a semantic artifice, as we clearly have solved difficult problems and continue to do so repeatedly. However, we feel so strongly about our highly successful approach to solving problems that we insist our long history of solving difficult problems is nothing but a record of solving lots and lots of little problems we had decomposed from the big, bad, difficult problems.

- It bears repeating. If you want to be a successful problem solver, you must break up difficult problems into pieces, and work on the piece you understand best. This takes a combination of patience and trust - patience in the process and trust in yourself. You have to have the patience to make incremental progress against a difficult problem, and the trust that you and your team members will learn from each step forward and gain insights into the remainder of the problem. Attempting to solve a difficult problem all at once usually results in failure, as poor assumptions and insufficient expertise are applied to designing fundamentally flawed solutions.

> *If you want to be a successful problem solver, you must break up difficult problems into pieces, and work on the piece you understand best.*

Ask yourself how many times you have assembled a team to solve a problem and every team member knew everything there was to know about the problem. Never, right? That's a prototypical difficult problem solving experience. Despite everyone's best efforts and intentions, excellent alternatives to effectively and efficiently solve a problem are overlooked during the course of a project. We feel this is not a fault of the project team, but rather the fault of the objectives set at the outset of the project. When success is defined as, "Get it done, get it all done.", or words to that effect, project teams naturally focus on whatever techniques and knowledge they have at the outset of the project, set a course, and execute it to the best of their abilities. This often results in a team that is over-extended, frustrated, and unable to achieve the goals that management has set out for them.

The preferred alternative to over-extending a team and frustrating them by requiring they solve the entirety of a difficult problem is to allow them to make progress where they are both comfortable and certain of making progress. Teams are inspired by this kind of management flexibility and awareness, as everyone likes to be part of a team that achieves, a team that succeeds. As they get smarter, the team members will bring ideas and new, innovative approaches to their managers on how to solve subsequent phases of the difficult problem.

Once your team members learn to solve problems through incremental innovation, they can then apply that skill to solving other complex problems. When teams and employees are taught to solve problems in this way, every worker in every role will be able to think of complex problems as tractable, as long as a realistic, incremental problem solving approach is used. This applies most of all to the highly-educated employees who have been taught to solve problems by delivering a single, monolithic 100% solution. This is a natural derivative of the academic experience carried over to the business or government world. Most educational systems teach case studies in solving projects that are bite-sized and tractable.. While this focus on simple solutions skills is incredibly useful at making progress on projects, the mindset of seeking the 100% solution in all cases turns out to be harmful whenever a difficult or Wicked Problem is encountered.

In most cases, 5/67 Problem Solving and the thinking that goes along with it, is an eye-opener for many people with extensive formal educations. They have learned a variety of techniques and methods for analysis, had little to no practical problem solving experience before starting work, and have long been accustomed to seeking 100% solutions from the beginning. The very existence of Gantt Charts planning out all the steps of a project from day one are testament to this kind of thinking.

> *Most educational systems teach case studies in solving projects that are bite-sized and tractable. ...the mindset of seeking the 100% solution in all cases turns out to be harmful whenever a difficult or Wicked Problem is encountered...*

A fundamental reason why incremental progress and iterative problem solving is so much more effective than a "Big Bang" project approach is due to learning. Simply put, old ideas and methods often won't solve new problems. As project team members learn, they develop new ideas and methods, which allow more aspects of the problem to be address. We like to use the following cartoon to make a point here.

How do we take the next Step?

We want to figure out how to make the big leap, tackling the solution in one big step. The reality is, big leaps are really just a series of improvements and insights that result in new ideas and methods.

CHAPTER 4

5/67 Tools: The Yes/No Chart

One of the key issues that we faced early in our 5/67 Problem Solving was addressing the issue of "action" in the workplace. This is action that is needed to accomplish a task. In that light, we defined the work of an organization as "planning, controlling and doing" the work. And in defining control: it was measuring the work and then adjusting as needed. All this made sense when people just did their work. If they needed help on improving their processes, we could do that. We are good at that. We could help them improve how they ran their machine or operated the computer in a billing department. After all, these were processes and we are process improvement experts.

But what do you do when the person that was suppose to do the work, didn't "want" to do it or saw no reason to do it or comply with a time constraint that was critical to the overall success of the organization. And there was no measure of how to do that. How do you get someone to comply with a schedule time constraint? And then further, what do you do when the Boss's son is lazy and is delaying shipments of product by not responding to the required time table of the organization.

That is the problem that we faced in one of our early projects.

And so, we combined the "No Blame" Mantra with the "Yes/No" Metric and ended up with the "Yes/No Chart." The No Blame was key here. If we are going to measure a team, there was No Blame for the result. It was measurement without blame. "Change without reprisal." We don't care about excuses or reasons why something is not done - period. Either is was done or not done. There was no ambiguity in the measurement.

When this is a problem, we usually find this during the "Root Cause Analysis Phase" of our problem solving process. What is the reason that this problem is causing waste?

For instance, an individual does not want to do something that s/he needs to do, for whatever reason. And rather than point blame at the problem individuals, we needed a way to "awaken" them to the "folly of their ways." In this context, a Yes/No chart is a simple tool that clearly communicates to the entire team (not just an individual) regarding the success or failure of a specific objective. For example, did the delivery truck leave on time today? (see chart)

Did the truck leave on time?

Mon	Tue	Wed	Thu	Fri
X	X	X	O	O

Was the advertising copy submitted on time? Did the production run achieve 100% defect-free quality and deliver the product on schedule? Such highly visible charts can galvanize a team into focusing on a problem in a way that common management directives cannot. And it is unambiguous because the answers are "Yes" or "No". "Maybe" is not an option and the whole process is protected with No Blame. Notice also that we did not create a "Yes/No Chart" that said, "Did Charlie (the truck driver), leave on time?"s In other words, we don't measure an individual, we measure an event for a team.

The way that this idea developed has a funny history. At one of our early War on Waste pilot companies, we had talked about No Blame and someone in the class raised the issue of the truck leaving late every day. The minute that was mentioned a hush went over the room. As we delved into the root cause, somewhat naively, we knew something was going on. There was even some tittering. So why was there a problem when the truck leaves late? What was the root cause?

So what was going on here? To get to the bottom of this problem we went out to the shipping area and put up the first

Yes/No chart. It looked something like the chart above.

It was done on a sheet of flip-chart paper and was done so that anyone passing by the area could see it. As we walked by the area with the CEO one evening, as we often do to point out issues employees had raised, he noticed the chart. He asked what it was about. We told him that the employees had identified the importance of the truck leaving on time. If it left after 9:00 AM, it couldn't complete its rounds to the San Jose area from the North Bay and get back before the heavy commute and end up with lots of overtime for the driver.

We looked at the chart with the CEO and there were three big red X's on the chart. The red X indicates "No" in response to the posted question: Did the truck leave before 9:00 AM? And no one wants to get red X's. So when we investigated the root cause, it turned out that the CEO's son was not getting at 6:30 AM, to do the inspections necessary to get the parts loaded on the truck and get it out before 9:00 AM. Once the explanation was on the table, the son got in on time, the parts were inspected and the truck left before 9:00 AM. From that moment forward, the Yes/No chart had earned its merits as a valuable measuring technique.

We have used the Yes/No Chart at a number of companies to manage the truck schedule. In all of those situations when we arrived, the truck was rarely leaving on time, for any number of reasons. And they are usually very good reasons. Again, before the yes/no chart goes up, it must be determined that it is important that the truck leaves by a particular time. Why measure something if there are no consequences from not leaving on time? That is, if the consequences for leaving on time are no different than those for not leaving on time, this is not the right issue to measure. The individuals or departments affected by the truck's schedule must agree that a measurement is appropriate. However, once the yes/no chart goes up, there are no excuses and No Blame is the rule.

We should point out here that we have not found that it is

particularly effective to focus on individuals or to attempt to modify behavior directly. Rather than focusing on an individual, it is important to focus on what work is done. Additionally, it is often more useful to focus on the output of an individual's work group than on the work of an individual.

We have used the Yes/No Chart continuously over the last 30 years. Some examples follow:

1. Company Can't Ship Orders on Time: A small company had a long-standing and costly problem; it couldn't manage to ship orders on time. The root cause of the problem boiled down to a major disagreement between individuals in different departments about what constituted an order and who could make a commitment to ship a product by a particular date. For example, if employee A committed inventory from the MRP system to a client, it was expected to ship that day. But another employee B might have a client with a need for the same product. Even if he could see that the item was in the system but committed to another client, he would ignore this. He would go down to the material warehouse and remove the item, put it with a few other items of the order and put it on the shipping table. Now we had a late order. The one from Employee A. This was a big issue because they had about 10 major customers (5% of their 200 customers) that generated 90% of their business. So on any day, they shipped 200 to 350 orders and on an average 30% of their orders were late. They had 10 major customers that accounted for 90% of their orders. So on any day all ten customers would have a late shipment. It was so bad, that one of the employees with less than sterling character noted, "it really is a wonder we have any customers." When the CEO heard this, he lamented to me, "if he thinks we are bad, we are really bad." When he heard all the stuff going on, and we do find out about all that stuff, he decided that he wanted this problem solved immediately.

We discussed the problem with the team working on the issue and settled on using the yes/no chart as the means to attack the problem. The chart asked a simple question: "Did all orders ship on time?" The results were reported by the person most likely to have the information, the guy on the shipping dock; he knew what had been shipped. The President promised a pizza party for everyone if they shipped all the orders on time.

A simple chart was prepared, and "no's" were recorded for fourteen days in a row. However, on the fifteenth day, a "yes" appeared, indicating shipping success! (See attached chart!)

Did all orders ship on time?

8-Sep	9-Sep	10-Sep	11-Sep	12-Sep	15-Sep	16-Sep	17-Sep	18-Sep	19-Sep	On time Shipments
X	X	X	X	X	X	X	X	X	X	0
22-Sep	23-Sep	24-Sep	25-Sep	26-Sep	29-Sep	30-Sep	1-Oct	2-Oct	3-Oct	
X	X	X	X	O	X	X	O	O	O	4
6-Oct	7-Oct	8-Oct	9-Oct	10-Oct	13-Oct	14-Oct	15-Oct	16-Oct	17-Oct	
X	X	O	X	X	O	O	O	O	O	6

The President should have been happy about this. He had to buy pizza when they succeeded. He didn't mind that but he suspected something was wrong. He investigated and found out that the guy on the shipping dock had shipped 310 orders on time. One of the last few items was going to be 5 days late. So he made it 6 days late by shipping it on Monday. The President laughed because the employees had won. But he raised the bar, pizza only happened with 3 days in a row to get around the earlier problem. On the next Friday, they won again. He raised the bar to earn pizza to 5 days in a row and the employees got it after the 6th week. From that point forward they didn't miss a shipment for 8 months.

This example drives home the main message of our measurement philosophy: **Measure the problem. Measure it simply. Post it for all to see.** In the example just cited, no one, including the president, expected a "yes" to appear for several months. After all, the problem had been around for years. The fact that the "yes's" began on the fifteenth day was more than encouraging; it got everybody in the company excited that they could perform as a team to solve the problem. Everyone knew the goal of the company was to ship 100% of the orders on time. There was No Blame for failure but then again there were to be No Excuses.

As a corollary to this issue, when we begin assignments, we are often told that the company has high absenteeism, low morale, etc. We are then asked, "What are you going to do about it?" And we answer, typically, "Nothing." We don't solve problems directly; we help other people solve problems. If we solve the problems, we are the ones who are learning. We want our clients to learn to solve problems using our concepts. So, we assure that the burden of solving organizational problems is on the shoulders of the client employees; in our experience, they always find a way to solve the problems. In all cases, measurement is the key to solving these problems. And because of that morale improves and high absenteeism improves. It becomes fun to work at a company that is winning in the market. It is not fun to be part of a loser (that can't ship orders on time).

2. Field Plant-Care Technicians never called in on time

A final example is one of our favorites. One of our early clients was a plant-care company. Each of the field Plant-care Technicians was supposed to call into the Nursery to schedule pickup of plants that needed to be delivered to their clients the following day. These Plant-care Technicians were field personnel who were out in the field taking care of plants and flowers placed in corporate facilities around the San Francisco Bay Area. These people were to call the nursery by 10:00 AM the day before their scheduled pick up day at the headquarters. In all there were 13 such technicians in the field and their calls were distributed to different days of the week.

The rules were very simple. They had to call before 10:00 AM, not 10:01 AM. The data of the first four weeks is noted in the chart below. You will note that of the 52 different calls that were to be made by 13 technicians over 4 weeks that 26/52 calls were not made on time. That is, they were late 50% of the time.

Did the plant tech call before 10:00 AM and talk to the Nursery Supervisor about the next day's plant requirements?

Technician	1	2	3	4	5	6	7	8	9	10	11	12	13	Late Calls 1st 4 weeks	Late Calls 2nd 4 weeks
Week 1	X	X	O	X	X	O	O	X	X	O	X	X	X	9	
Week 2	O	X	X	O	O	X	X	X	O	X	O	O	O	6	
Week 3	X	O	O	X	O	X	O	O	X	O	X	O	X	6	
Week 4	O	X	X	O	X	O	X	X	O	O	O	O	O	5	
Week 5	O	O	O	O	O	O	O	O	O	O	O	O	O		0
Week 6	O	O	O	O	O	O	X	O	O	O	O	X	O		2
Week 7	O	O	O	O	O	O	O	O	O	O	O	O	O		0
Week 8	O	O	O	O	O	O	O	O	O	O	O	O	O		0
Total Late Calls	2	3	2	2	2	2	3	3	2	2	2	2	2	26	2
Percentage Late Calls														(50%)	(4%)

They got a red X if they didn't get to the nursery person by 10:00 AM. A number of the technicians made their calls at 9:57 AM, got through to the operator before 10:00 AM but were put on hold while the nursery manager got to the phone. By the time the manager got on the line, it was after 10:00 AM. This resulted in their failure to report on time and put an "X" on the day's results.

(And this all happened in the days before cell phones were available to the plant techs. They had to find phone booths or other remote phones to call in to the office.)

Guess what? The next time they called they did so with enough time to spare so that they weren't late again.

This is a very powerful tool of measurement and it generates positive results very quickly.

At the end of the month, the results of the first 4 weeks were discussed and the employees got real mad when the results showed their failures. The group had done very badly. The owner of the business went ballistic when she saw the results. They were posted every day and she just never looked at them. So one of the major things that I got from this was that if you post the results, keep tabs on them every day and provide appropriate feedback to get the results that you want. Don't wait until the end of the month to remind the CEO to look at the results. If you are playing a game, you want to know the score immediately. Posting them and then discussing them 4 weeks after the action would be like a baseball scorekeeper getting in touch with a baseball player 4 weeks after a game and telling him that he lost. Who cares at that point? Make the results known immediately.

Anyway, after calming the owner down, we set a goal to improve the results and surprisingly of the 52 calls made in the next 4 weeks only 2 failed to meet the goal. Impressive? Certainly, but it is not an unusual result. It just works.

CHAPTER 5

5/67 Tools: $50 / $500 / $5000 Task Log

One of our favorite tools to create 5/67 awareness is using the 50/500/5000 task log. This is a tool that is designed to get our clients to understand whether they are spending their time strategically, creating the most value for their business. Or, are they frequently engaged in managerial or administrative tasks which make the executive feel like he or she is making progress, but in reality the organization is either standing still or falling behind.

A 50/500/5000 task log is a mechanism to record what was done during each period of time throughout several consecutive workdays. Every task must be assigned a $50, $500, or $5000 value, those number selected to approximate administrative, managerial or strategic tasks. Clients quickly realize when they are wasting their time, doing low value activities, or not focusing on what is really important.

So, what are these $50, $500, and $5000 tasks? The notion is the hourly benefit to the organization associated with the work performed. Of course, the numbers are merely conceptual placeholders to get our attention, for if the CEO of Walmart is working on a $5000/hr task, he is truly wasting his time! Some examples:

- **$50 (administrative)**: document filing, processing emails, returning calls from unknown callers, reviewing the work priorities of competent managers and employees

- **$500 (managerial)**: Contract reviews, performance reviews, project management sessions

- **$5000 (strategic)**: Planning, offsite retreats, peer networking, reading/learning, challenging their team to find more efficient, effective solutions to their problem or project.

We like to say that the management of time spent on administrative, managerial, and strategic tasks is the "CEO Process", or, the method by which a CEO performs his/her responsibilities in running an organization. This "CEO Process" is one that is not well-defined, typically, when a CEO takes over or starts a company. We have found that there is almost always a great deal of room for improvement in the "CEO Process" for our CEO clients.

The reason that we use the 50/500/5000 dollars per hour notion is to create understanding amongst our clients of the value of their time. If we tell them to note down administrative, managerial, and strategic work, we rarely get good data. If we ask them if they are spending their time administratively, managerially, or strategically, almost all executives will say they are mostly strategic. However, most people who are involved in a business, whether it be for-profit, government, or charity, have a decent understanding of the dollar value contribution of any given task. Thus, when we ask for logs of their $50/$500/$5000 per hour work, we get really accurate information.

Most executives initially strenuously object to this "administrative" task of logging their time, thinking there is no value, and, in fact, we are "forcing" $50/hr tasks on them! They usually cite a number of reasons why they don't need to monitor their time:

1. They believe they already spend their time wisely.

2. They do not believe that our 50/500/5000 log tool can help them at all

3. Some even say, "You don't know my business, why are we bothering with this?

We always persist in this argument, because we know from experience that this task logging activity is one of the most strategic things an executive can do. Why? Because maximizing your time spent working on $5000 items in your daily routine are key to being a successful CEO. Ultimately most every client gives in and accepts the task, usually for a shorter period than we desire. Typically they will log the time for one day and then review it with us. After that short review, the response is almost always the same. "There is no way I'm that inefficient! Let's do this for several more days."

We do our best to suppress our grins at this point, as we knew this moment was coming.

Yet, after compiling the log, every single executive is astonished at how much time they waste on activities that could easily be delegated to others, and how much opportunity there is for improvement in their daily activities. They find a remarkable amount of $50/hr tasks, most of which they can pass on to others. Yet, these executive clients sometimes find it hard to give up these tasks, as they are easy to do, require little thinking, and are part of their daily routine. Nevertheless, increasing the time on $5000/hr tasks always leads to better "CEO Process" and better overall company performance. In the end, the 50/500/5000 tool is a way to get managers and executives to focus on the aspects of organizational problems which will lead to 5/67 solutions. We have learned from our consulting experience that the 50/500/5000 task log in an important aspect of adjusting management and executive thinking to the 5/67 Thinking mode.

CHAPTER 6

5/67 Speed Analysis

The main point of 5/67 Speed Analysis was noticed when we were rushing to complete projects. We didn't have enough time so instead of trying to get 20% of the effort to get 80% of the benefit, we just said, get 5% of the benefit and see what happens. And we got 60% to 75% of the benefit consistently, which we called "the 5/67 Rule." This enabled us to do speedy analyses of problems because when you compared the time to define 5% of the effort versus 20% of the effort, a lot of time was saved.

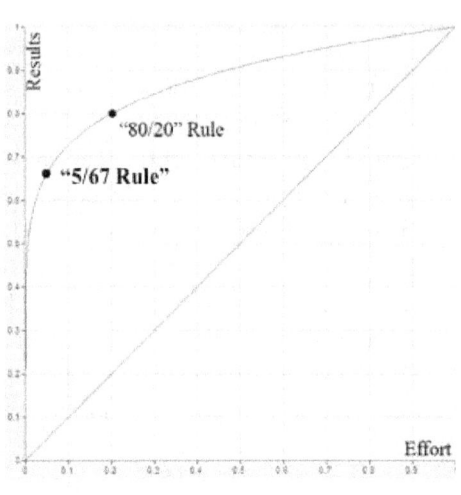

If you look at the curve, you notice that 5/67 fits nicely on the curve. It is in the steep part of the curve where a little change in the effort returns a lot of benefit. When we first plotted the 5/67 results we also notice that there was greater leverage in 5/67 vs 20/80, 13x versus 4x. So you get 3 times the leverage by doing 5/67 implementations. And we see that kind of result all the time.

We are interested in moving our projects along as fast as we can. Using 5/67 Thinking gives us the speed that we demand.

In an example that we have used elsewhere, a team was working on a problem that involved a problem with invoices. They saw that they needed to do some analysis to prove their point. Everyone was telling them to collect 20% of the data for a year which would have been a large number of invoices. And it would have taken them too long. 20% of a year's invoices in this case would have amounted to 6000 invoices. They did only 2% and even that was too much for them but they did the job of looking for problem invoices in 2 man hours. If they had done 20% they would have taken 20 hours and we only had 4 weeks of classes of 1.5 hours per class. So 20% wasn't going to work. We did 1 week's worth of data or 2% and got a number that the CEO thought was about right. So we ran with that number. It wasn't 5% but it worked.

And whether it was high or low was irrelevant, it gave us a number that we could use for further analysis and we completed the problem resolution and a proposed solution in time to make the presentation to the CEO on Monday of the 5th (fifth) week of the War on Waste Training.

Conclusion: Collect a little data, in 5/67 Thinking, 5% of the total targeted data, and incorporate that data into a proposal that sizes the extent of the problem. And you will be pleased with the result and the speed by which you got there.

CHAPTER 7

5/67 Projects: Starting is Better than Being Right

Most of our clients suffer from the paralysis of analysis. They want to know exactly what is going to happen at every step of a large-scale project before they are willing to start. Without this visibility into every step of a project, these clients feel they are not planning properly, or managing the project correctly, or something like that. This is contrary to 5/67 Thinking, and definitely contrary to achieving success in dealing with difficult problems or Wicked Problems.

The key to success in project execution is to start on a reasonable path, make progress, and allow your project team to get smarter and more insightful about the problem they are solving. As we have stated before, project teams just do not have 100% of all the skills and insights necessary to efficiently execute a difficult project when they first start. It's actually irrational to believe that they do. This is because many problems are challenging (either difficult problems or Wicked Problems) and are not susceptible to easy solutions.

All projects are just a series of problems to be solved. For example, the incremental problems to be solved might be design problems, resource assignment problems, financial allocation problems, partner and external factor problems, and time and scheduling problems. All of these have to be resolved while working towards the goal of a successful project outcome. The reader may want to pause here and consider if they have ever had a project team that tackled a difficult problem which, at the outset, was 100% prepared for every problem they encountered along the way?

5/67 Thinking says, define a successful outcome very clearly, communicate it to your team, get their agreement and buy-in, then just let them start. And, do so in a work environment where incremental progress is celebrated, the definition of success isn't changed as the project moves along, and the team is supported by management throughout the project. This iterative, incremental progress approach is an ideal way to solve difficult problems.

Thus, a key to having a world-class problem solving team is to have leadership which prefers an intelligent start on the most tractable aspect of the problem rather than forcing a team to develop an entire solution at the outset and demand they follow their Project Gantt Chart every step of the way as a means of project management.

What are the specific steps for a manager, leader, or executive to go through to ensure this ideal way to tackle difficult problems? There are three keys to starting on the right path and making incremental progress on a difficult problem:

1. **Define Success**. A clear definition of an overall successful outcome serves as a guiding light to a project team. The team knows the goal, so they can intelligently combine their expertise to develop an initial approach. Further, much like navigating through a dark tunnel, having a light at the end keeps the team more or less headed in the right direction. The clear definition of success serves as the beacon for any project team.

2. **Get Inputs from your Team**. It is amazing how many executives believe that only a team of "super-educated" managers or supervisors should be queried to develop a problem-solving strategy. Perhaps such leaders believe that only other executives and leaders have this responsibility and authority. However, our experience shows that the staff who work most closely in the problem area tend to have the best insights, especially on an initial approach. The staff with the daily work experience related to the project and problem at hand, in reality, are the most "super educated" of anyone in your company, irrespective of how many college degrees they happen to have.

3. **Create a Positive Environment**. Create one where

incremental success and innovation are celebrated. Acknowledge the problem is challenging. Encourage ideas and ensure nobody is criticized for an idea that isn't accepted: No Blame[1] Ideas without reprisal. Allow mistakes to occur as learning experience. Learn the concept of "Failing Forward" as a mantra to encourage your teams to put forth ideas and feel safe while doing so.

As a corollary to this idea, one of the authors had a mentor who was a former CEO of a large international company and he believed that he was doing a good job if he was right on 50% of his project ideas. He felt that as he watched ideas emerge on a project that was failing to meet expectations, he didn't kill these projects, he just reduced the amount of money he was expending on the idea. His mantra was, "feed the winners, starve the losers." The losers sometimes found ways to escape starvation. And it was those ideas that he was most excited about because they showed that sometimes, timing is wrong or the initial understanding of an idea was incorrect and mid-course corrections were necessary.

An example of two different approaches to approach the same problem may be illustrative. We once were part of a team of two that took on the challenge of building a highly reliable, scalable system to process an as-yet unproven trading algorithm. Unbeknownst to us, the brokerage had another formal development team taking on the same challenge at the same time.

Here were the requirements, in summary:

- **Algorithmic correctness**: This system had to get the right answer under all trading and quote conditions, which was a challenge itself.

- **Reliable**: The system had to be 100% reliable during the trading day. No single point failures.

- **Scalable**: The system had to handle a large number of

---

1 No Blame - the logo is a registered trademark of the War on Waste Academy

trading algorithm "matching sets" without any loss of performance.

- **Schedule**: The system needed to be brought online within 6 months.

The results are a case study in 95/33 Thinking versus 5/67 Thinking. The two man team solved the problem in 3 months and were successful with the system. The large, formal team never actually finished the project, as they came up with an incredibly complex design to meet all four requirements at the same time. That team was ultimately disbanded and reassigned to other projects.

The software developer and one of the authors simply ignored the last three requirements and tried to get the algorithm to work. That took quite a few weeks with a number of mistakes, and restarts along the way. But, we got there, And, in so doing, we realized that there was no dependency between the algorithm and the quote service (an insight), and we could simple duplicate the traffic on the network (a tool) to populate two servers at the same time with the same information. So, the solution to the second problem just fell into our lap because of lessons we learned while solving the 5/67 aspect of the problem. Another week and that requirement was dealt with. When we turned our attention to scalability, we found that the system already could process almost 4,000 different match sets, which was more than the customer actually needed. So, a careful measurement revealed that once we had the first two aspects of the difficult problem solved, the third and fourth requirements were really just Stupid Problems.

The most important take-away from this chapter is to avoid insisting on an overall "total" solution from a team. The authors understand that doing so fosters a "can't do" environment, as demanding a total solution to a difficult problem brings into play two of the "Deadly Demotivators". First is the "Goal Too Far" demotivator where a team just won't give their best efforts because they know the approach is unrealistic. Second is "Unrealistic Expectations" where teams get frustrated because a manager or leader is asking for something that clearly cannot be accomplished as stated. We summarize this kind of management failure as "95/33 Thinking" which we will discuss later.

Allow your teams to make realistic progress. Celebrate learning and growth and progress. Mistakes along the way are less impactful, because the project has been approached incrementally. Thus, mistakes are really just learning opportunities for everyone.

CHAPTER 8

Good Enough Is, The 5/67 Mantra

One of the greatest obstacles to successful projects and problem-solving is the desire to get the outcome "exactly" right. Many executives and managers want to do as well as they possibly can in every endeavor. In other words, they are pursuing the best possible outcome and do so in all cases. American business culture tends to celebrate this kind of fastidious attention to maximizing product, project, or business results. For example, Steve Jobs' has been repeatedly lauded for sending projects back to redesign some aspect of a product until the product was "just right".

While both authors had the chance to work with Steve Jobs, and have the utmost respect for his estimable career accomplishments, we find this kind of quest for perfection to be almost universally harmful to all kinds of organizations. We both discourage and reject this pursuit of perfection because it almost always de-motivates employees, confuses project teams, and represents classic "95/33 Thinking". Thus, we coined the grammatically deficient expression "Good Enough Is", as it best captures the proper mindset for defining success in solving a problem.

First, some explanation is in order regarding why seeking perfection is such a harmful strategy for an executive, manager, or leader. One of the four great de-motivators is called, "Moving the goalposts". This is a tactic used by managers, often those seeking a perfect outcome, wherein the definition of success keeps changing. This causes team members to become frustrated, which in turns leads to a drop in effort. Nobody likes to successfully finish a task only to be told, "Oh, sorry, you aren't done."

The reason "Good Enough Is" is important is because it exemplifies a basic requirement in problem-solving, which is to pick a realistic goal. Further, in order for problem-solvers to be productive and efficient, it is equally important to define success clearly. Putting these two together, you logically get "Good Enough Is". For example, if a factory has a 2% defect rate and a 0.5% defect rate is acceptable, then that is the goal. That is good enough. "Good Enough Is!" While it may be tempting to seek an absolutely perfect 0.0% defect rate, or the goal of 6-Sigma, in fact, that would be defining the unachievable as the project goal, and that would tremendously demotivate the team.

We had a client with a high-pressure container product manufactured from the output of two assembly lines that had a major defect and net-production problem. They simply were not getting a high enough product yield to be profitable as a business despite solid product demand from their customer base. There was simply too much waste in defective products and customer returns. Further, the management had a commissioned consulting report that entailed an elegant design to produce new assembly lines, optimized process analysis, and an expanded capacity that would solve all of their problems. The solution outlined in the report looked beautiful, read nicely, and was commensurately expensive.

Fortunately, this client asked us to examine the problem before spending the vast sum of money required to build entirely new assembly lines, retrain all of their workers, and restart their production. Within a day or two we realized that merely slowing the faster of the two assembly lines would avoid the production defect problem and improve net production, because 100% of the defects were coming from the intermediate components of the faster line, and then only for those intermediate components that were set aside while awaiting the slower production line.. The cost of our solution was only a few thousand dollars. By balancing the two production lines we eliminated their primary source of defects and the yields were sufficient to meet existing demand with almost no defects.

Only later did we bother to consider how to improve production output by speeding up both lines while maintaining quality standards. One of our War on Waste projects successfully produced some superb ideas from the employees which allowed us to achieve a nice improvement in output.

We applied 5/67 Thinking. While it was desirable to achieve zero defects and much higher output, we declined to address those problems at first. We noticed that the simplest thing we could do was slow down the line that was building up excess intermediate component inventory. We realized everyone would gain insights and have ideas later on how to increase production capacity.

Perhaps one of the best modern examples of 5/67 Thinking in corporate America is Google. Why is Google so good at 5/67?

- They try things out. Google is completely willing to make mistakes and learn from them. They just don't like to make huge mistakes, which shows they have an aversion to 95/33 thinking.

- They kill products when they think they aren't right, or can be improved, often to the dismay of their customers at the time. The authors bemoaned the elimination of Google Desktop Search for many months until we realized that, yes, Google was right. Important unstructured data was all going to the cloud anyway, so Google Desktop Search wasn't needed any longer.

- Google knows that a little progress each time results in a great result in the long run

- They don't care that they make mistakes along the way. Google is happy to learn from mistakes

So, back to the famous Steve Jobs. Why was Jobs able to succeed despite his constant demand for perfection? Jobs had created and fostered a very special environment at Apple Computer that will rarely be repeated. First, Apple had a strong culture of innovation. The culture accepted trying and making product mistakes, like the Lisa or the Newton, even if an unsuccessful presentation to Jobs was a painful experience for the employees. Second, everyone knew that Jobs would provide the resources necessary to continue work on a product that he deemed not quite ready. So, Apple didn't have the resource constraints that virtually every company has. Last, and most importantly, the teams tacitly knew that a product completion presentation to Jobs wasn't really a completion presentation. It was a progress report. Jobs was almost certainly going to find new flaws, have new ideas, or make new suggestions on how to improve the product. After a painful few years, everyone accepted this going in that Jobs was demanding perfection. They had learned that painfully over the years. In addition, there was a tradition of celebrating product roll outs and design successes at Apple, which helped maintain spirit and motivation for employees as they iteratively improved products until the Jobs stamp of approval could be obtained.

At the War on Waste Academy, we don't believe many companies have done the groundwork that Jobs did to create such a fertile environment for innovation and 5/67-type iteration. And, there are precious few companies in the entire world with the available talent and financial resources that Apple Computer had and continues to have. Thus, eschew seeking perfection and accept that "Good Enough Is". Your business and your employees will all be more successful.

CHAPTER 9

Perfection is the Enemy of Good

In the last chapter we discussed setting goals that are realistic and achievable, and avoiding setting goals that are effectively unreachable. Here we will dive deeper into that topic to ensure that our problem-solving readers can understand just how dangerous the pursuit of perfection really is.

Consider this chart we showed earlier in the book. If you look closely at the green line, it is a graph of the results/benefits charted against effort. In other words, how much you get for how hard you work.

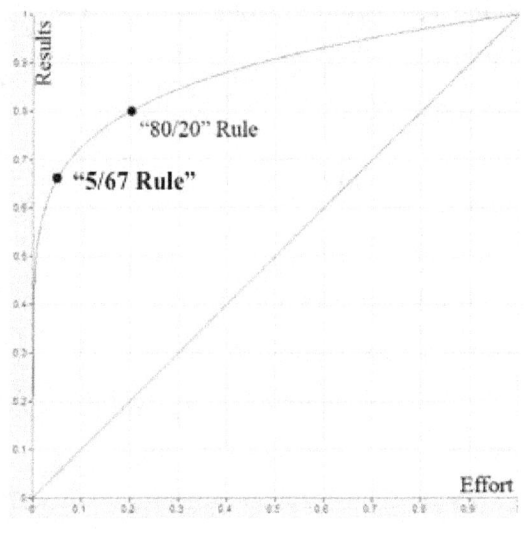

If you look at this green line carefully, you will see that the last 10% of benefit more than doubles the amount of effort. In reality that green line never really touches the 100% mark. It just gets closer and closer but never really gets there, which in mathematics is something called an "asymptote".

So, what does the green line have to do with projects, problem-solving, and, most importantly, "Perfection is the Enemy of Good"?. Several bad things happen when project leaders, executives, and managers set perfection as the required outcome in solving a problem. Teams get demotivated, people get frustrated, and businesses waste precious resources chases unachievable goals that, in most cases, weren't actually even necessary.

Imagine if every baseball pitcher was judged a failure if they did not pitch a perfect game with 27 consecutive strikeouts? Especially when giving up six or seven hits and a few runs will yield a pitching win most of the time? i.e. "Good Enough Is".

We had the opportunity to work on the Toyota Production System during its formative years. One of the early issues that we had with the Toyota Production System was the Japanese Zen philosophy and its constant striving for perfection. When you do problem solving with 5/67 Thinking, there is no search for perfection. It is, as noted in the previous chapter, getting things moving, learn from mistakes, avoid wasting resources, and embrace that "Good Enough Is". So, we strove to teach Toyota, and we strive to teach all our customers, that the only real way to consistently improve is to iteratively do 5/67 projects and consistently achieve better and better results.

There are four deadly de-motivators in organizational behavior:

1. Information overload
2. Insufficient organizational support
3. A goal too far, AKA unrealistic expectations
4. Moving the goalposts, or changing the definition of success after starting

The pursuit of perfection is the manifestation of deadly demotivator number 3, "A goal too far". Our employees and team members know their jobs and know what can and cannot be done. Sometimes they know this overtly and other times intuitively, but they know. When a goal is set that requires perfection, these same intelligent and capable teammates immediately lose hope of achieving success. They know that the goal is unachievable, so why bother working hard? This is the kind of goal-setting and project management which leads to perfunctory "punching the clock" kinds of work habits from the team.

Further, setting the perfect solution as your goal absolutely guarantees your team will never achieve success. This leads to excessive spending, team frustration, and wasted resources expended on an objective that most likely was not a business necessity in the first place. Going back to our baseball analogy, .300 hitters and 2.0 ERA pitches are failing quite a bit and are among the top performers in their profession. They are clearly good enough.

To avoid the "Perfection is the Enemy of Good" problem, define your problems and your Definition of Success very carefully. What result will achieve the business goal? For example, in a sales management situation we all would like 100% closes on all of our accounts for all of our sales reps. But that level of perfection is a fantasy. What is realistic? What achieves the business growth objectives? Perhaps a 40% overall close rate will exceed the business revenue objectives. The point is to set your goals according to what is best aligned with the overall business or organizational strategy. As a corollary, whenever a goal or objective sounds like achieving perfection, rethink your objective.

CHAPTER 10

How to Solve Wicked Problems

Wicked Problems are the most complex and difficult problems of all. We encounter these problems from time to time in business, in government, and in life. Wicked Problems have the attribute that both ill-advised and well-intended changes can easily make the problem worse, not better. Most Wicked Problems have been in existence for quite a long period of time, and are thus considered intractable problems. Examples of Wicked Problems include government budgeting, improving corporate PR, solving homelessness, setting foreign policy, and many military strategy issues. Examples of actually exacerbating a Wicked Problem abound in these and other sectors, all due to an incorrect approach to solving these Wicked Problems.

Pulling harder won't unravel the knot

Wicked Problems are not stupid problems with simple solutions, nor difficult problems where the wrong approach merely means some small initial waste and learning occurred. For stupid problems a very simple, economical solution will make the problem go away. The direct decomposition and iterative approach with 5/67 Thinking solves a difficult problem. Neither approach is adequate for Wicked Problems.

Wicked Problems are far more challenging than difficult problems. In order to take on a Wicked Problem without making it worse, the problem solver must artfully and carefully measure relevant information about the problem and gain insights on how to safely begin to attack the problem. This requirement is really what differentiates our approach to Wicked Problems from that of a difficult problem. Difficult problems are easy to decompose. Wicked Problems are not.

The fundamental challenge here is that teams taking on Wicked Problems really want to hurry up and show results. Getting results is the classic American business ethos. Show your manager that you are on your way to solving a problem and you can get organizational support. Thus, a paradox exists because this rush-to-action Wicked Problem approach inevitably creates even more problems due to the rush to action.

We have been asked to solve a few Wicked Problems in our consulting practice. One such case serves as a nice example of the proper approach. In order to solve this Wicked Problem we had to avoid several very likely and undesirable side effects. We could not increase costs in the existing core business, safety levels had to continue to be excellent or even improve, and a wholesale rebuilding of the business operations was not an option due to cost and adverse impact effects on the existing business.

Our client was a distribution and logistics operation. This distribution and logistics organization was being asked to support several new types of customers, all of which were very different than their long-standing traditional customer base. The delivery sizes were much smaller, deliveries were more frequent, and the product delivery schedule was relatively unpredictable. The existing business was quite predictable. Deliveries were large, easily scheduled, and the product mix was known in advance. Supporting the new customer types might be properly viewed as an entirely new business superimposed on the older one.

Several small pilot attempts had already been made at specific distribution centers, all of which had resulted in either higher costs, unacceptable small customer delivery performance, or increased risk of safety issues. The customer had tried segmenting the distribution center, had tried different pick/load forklifts and scheduling, and tried to manage their supply chain to push the problem upstream to their manufacturers. None of these approaches worked.

What was our approach? We went to several centers and watched their operations. Our objective was to learn how this distribution organization really worked and learn from the employees who made it work every day. After a few days we began to have ideas on how to "de-couple" the core large delivery business from the new, burgeoning small customer business. Some of the ideas were entirely ours, many were suggestions made by bright, capable employees we encountered, but almost all were a synthesis of the two sources.

Our key findings (measurements) that occurred during this observation phase were:

- The receiving and shelf-placement processes at these distribution centers were highly optimized. Any attempt to change these processes resulted in cost increases.

- The pick process was extremely hectic with forklifts and personnel constantly moving in high traffic areas in the warehouse. The proof of concept tests where changes were made to the pick process consistently resulted in safety hazards and productivity decreases due to forklift and personnel congestion in the warehouse corridors.

- The load process was uniquely separated from the other

processes at the distribution centers. One forklift with one operator was assigned to each truck. This proved to be our best starting point for incremental 5/67 Thinking solutions to the problem.

We had learned from the prior failures that product delivery from factories, product shelf placement, and product pick operations were incredibly sensitive. In other words, for this customer, the entire back end intake model was highly optimized. Any changes to accommodate the small customers resulted in negative business operation results for the core business. So, from careful measurement and operation we focused on the front end of the business - the loading of delivery trucks for customers.

This is when our Ah Ha! moment occurred. With some great suggestions from the lift and load operators, we realized that we could break up the pick-and-load operation into two parts. Pick the products from the shelves of the warehouses and drop them into intermediate work areas near the loading docks, then have front-end loaders which would take those products and pack the trucks for shipment. This idea had been considered in one form or another by the management team and discarded, because adding a process step almost always increases costs and reduces productivity. However, in this case, we found there was an optimization step possible in loading. We found a software package which informed the forklift operator how to best load the truck for each and every unique load. And, this software worked for any sized truck. The result was trucks were loaded much more quickly, which reduced costs. Secondly, by making loading separate from picking, we could optimize fragile versus non-fragile product placement in the trucks, which reduced the shipment breakage rate.

In the end, we made pick-to-load more expensive, but made load-to-delivery much more efficient, resulting in no overall loss in productivity. Sure, we would have loved to have found a clever approach to make everything 50% more efficient, but this business was already well run. Plus, our Definition of Success was to support small deliveries without increasing operation costs for the existing core business, and we achieved that.

Why did this project succeed? The number one reason was patience on the part of the executive management of our client. Without their support, none of this would have happened. They tolerated careful measurement and no discernible progress for many weeks while we learned enough to have insights into the Wicked Problem. The second, equally important reason, was that we asked a ton of questions and got a lot of great inputs from the employees at the distribution facilities. Their insights were a gold mine of ideas and information, all of which helped to shape our thinking.

At that point we approached this Wicked Problem like a difficult problem. We did a pilot of the two part pick-to-load process, debugged the software and system, tweaked the process, then rolled it out company-wide. Incremental progress resulted in learning, optimization, and an overall successful project.

If you want your organization to have the ability to take on Wicked Problems, ensure your teams carefully measure and assess the Wicked Problem to find an intelligent and useful initial approach that won't cause harm. Give them space too for measurement, learning and incremental success. Make sure to avoid demanding an overall solution by a certain time or certain date, but do demand clarity as to the Definition of Success for solving the problem. Request updates on what they have learned, their ideas, and their thinking as they progress. Make the process interactive and enjoyable. And, be sure to celebrate improved insights, small successes, and progress along the way to the overall solution.

Solving a Wicked Problems using yesterday's thinking and ideas almost always results in an unchanged or exacerbated problem. Had the aforementioned distribution company just picked a solution, perhaps an expensive system suggested by a warehouse management system vendor, they would have made the problem worse, and spent a lot of money doing so.

Wicked Problems are wicked because you can only solve a problem with what you know. For any problem, of any type, there is always new information to be learned about the problem that can help move a problem solver to a greater understanding of the problem. Once this new information is obtained, the problem takes on a new perspective because of greater insight. Every increment of learning helps move the problem understanding forward, and greater understanding of a problem's attributes results in better options for finding incremental solutions.

Wicked Problems have the attribute of "coming back to bite you" if you approach them too aggressively or without sufficient understanding. We see this regularly in large corporations and in government, where mistakes are made in solving problems that result in outcomes far worse than the original problem. We've seen this at Uber in dealing with corporate culture and productivity, Wells Fargo when trying to grow their account base, United Airlines with PR and customer service, and in many aspects of US government policies. An example from government is the program which spends vast amounts of taxpayer money to subsidize specific agricultural production such as ethanol from corn, which has the side effect of dramatically raising the cost of food for the entire population.

5/67 Thinking gives us the mindset for the right approach to solving Wicked Problems. Since these problems are too complex to fully analyze before starting, we accept this fact and use careful measurement and study to determine how to best start and make progress. Analyze and measure carefully before making any changes. Learning and gaining insights is far more important than rushing out and doing something.

Our guidance on addressing Wicked Problems is to spend a small amount of budget and resources and make progress towards a clearly-defined end goal. The team will get smarter about the Wicked Problem, they will learn, they will understand. Subsequent iterations of 5/67 project phases always make incremental progress. Ultimately, after a few iterations of 5/67 projects, a lot of progress has been made, or the problem has entirely been solved.

CHAPTER 11

95/33 Thinking: Your Government At Work

Since 5/67 Thinking is a key to project and decision success, it follows that 95/33 Thinking would provide the exact opposite type of results. And, in fact, 95/33 Thinking (the mathematical and logical opposite of 5/67), can be seen every day in "grand" projects in government and industry. There is a feeling of empowerment or relevance that seems to occur in managers who take on multi-million dollar projects with massive Gantt charts, huge project teams, and lofty goals. Yet, the actual results from these projects vary from mediocre to abjectly disappointing.

These leaders grow fond of "the big idea" and fund projects that are ill-conceived, overly complex, and poorly understood by the participants. Large corporations and national-level legislative policy often fits this description, and the results match what we expect. Their teams experience delays, are consistently over budget, and fall well short of desired results.

In our consulting practice we have found that "95/33 Thinking" is a nice term to capture traditional large organization thinking towards problem solving, and to further highlight how "5/67 Thinking" makes such a big difference. The "95/33 Thinking" term is an explicit reference to over-spending (95% of budget) to achieve little benefit (33%). Obviously, 95/33 is just subtracting 5/67 from 100/100.

Examples of this kind of traditional, unproductive thinking in problem solving abound. Major ERP implementations where tens of millions of dollars of license fees and implementation fees are expended only to result in an organization that is no more productive. In many cases the change management and process failures cause organizations to become less productive, so much so that they drop the ERP package entirely. We've seen these expensive ERP procurements and projects fail repeatedly within our customer base. Let's be clear - the issue isn't ERP systems, or the need large corporations have to centrally manage complex operations. Rather, the issue is the penchant for the project managers to define success as "get it all done now", rather than accept ERP implementations for the difficult problems that they are.

We find "95/33 Thinking" in government policy on a regular basis. Government agencies often adopt a "We must address the entire problem" posture without appropriate measurement, analysis, and acceptance that incremental progress is a good thing. The Obamacare overhaul of health insurance is an example. The legislation was drafted without sufficient subscriber, cost, or benefit analysis. As a result, insurance exchanges are failing as a result of this inadequate analysis of government administrative costs and acceptance of compulsory insured insurance rates.

The "War on Drugs" is another example of "95/33 Thinking" applied to a Wicked Problem. Unintended side effects wherein drug cartels and dealers simply adjusted their distribution and supply channel processes to get around US blockades and interdictions. In the end, drug prices rose and the illegal drug trade became more profitable, and thus more attractive. Commensurately drug related violence exploded in many parts of the southern USA, Mexico, Central America, and elsewhere. A perfect example of a poor approach to a Wicked Problem.

The common thread in these traditional problem solving techniques is an executive or management assumption to "solve this problem now!". Lack of acceptance of progress, insight, and learning inevitably lead to overly expensive project plans, implemented by teams that don't really understand the problem very well, and lead to poor or disastrous consequences.

CHAPTER 12

The No Blame Game: 5/67 Thinking Requires Ideas From Everyone

In our years of executing War on Waste programs, we have learned that the "No Blame Game" is perhaps the single most important aspect of 5/67 Thinking to achieve project and decision success. The reasons for this are fundamental to who we are as human beings. 5/67 types of projects tend to be started in a well-advised direction by a group of people who clearly understand the ultimate goal and are committed to the initial steps towards the solution. This only happens in an environment where past mistakes, poor practices, or inefficient processes have no repercussions on the team members responsible. That's "No Blame".

We require our client executive management to sponsor and support this concept throughout any of our War on Waste programs. It is a mandatory condition to have success in a project initiated using 5/67 Thinking, because nobody wants to be blamed for why a process is defective and unproductive. Because of this executive support, the teams come up with the best possible ideas, feel like they are part of the process, and readily buy into the solution the team ultimately develops. And they do this without fear of reprisal. The No Blame Game concept is very, very powerful.

In any company-wide project, all parts of the company are subject to review and considerations. No departments or processes are spared. In this kind of situation, many process inefficiencies in the business operation are exposed and many times feelings are tweaked. Tension can erupt and project disasters occur. This issue is calmed by "No Blame." With "No Blame" the special condition is created where it is OK to pass judgment on the inefficiencies of a neighboring department without hurt feelings or emotional repercussions. In fact, we believe so strongly in this concept that we trademarked "No

Blame."[2]

The trademark symbol is intended to symbolize to our clients and their employees that we are going to drive change at their company and we do it by invoking "No Blame." It is change without reprisal.

A comment is in order about how we began the No Blame Game. It started literally in the first War on Waste class at 6:30 AM at our first client. We were going over the meaning of the terms "waste" and "value-added" in the business process sense and the question was asked "Do you have any good examples of waste at this company?" A hand went up immediately. But before he answered, he turned around and looked around to the back of the rooms. That seemed odd at the time but he was looking to see if there was any managers in the back of the room.

If there were, he was going to keep his input to himself. It was too risky because, as was later discovered, the managers at this company were pretty brutal to anyone offering any unsolicited ideas for anything.

At that moment, the "No Blame Game" evolved and the logo emerged as the protection mantra of the suggested idea and we (the War on Waste Academy Team) were the enforcers of that concept. Note, we used the word "enforcer" here to illustrate what we had to do to make sure all ideas had an opportunity to be heard. And over 30 years, we have had great success supporting the implementation of over 10,000 ideas. And they

2 ® "No Blame" is a registered Trademark of War on Waste Academy & Len Bertain.

were all championed with the "No Blame Game."

We have found in all of our work that people want to help. They are willing to help. But they aren't going to help if it means that they are going to lose their job. This is a concern at all of the companies that we have delivered the War on Waste. People are insecure about offering ideas if their manager or foreman is going to make their life miserable. So the idea of "No Blame," or no reprisal, allows these folks to venture up to the table of risk and offer suggestions to eliminate waste. And when they are rewarded and praised for their ideas, boy is that ever exciting!

Perhaps the most important thing that can be pointed out about No Blame is this: the idea is the root of any change and NO BLAME protects the idea. This is like the freedom of speech. Without the freedom for people to assemble to listen to your free speech, free speech is neutered. No Blame then is to an idea, what freedom to assembly is to free speech. The US Bill of Rights was framed with a very simple understanding of what was necessary to insure a free democracy. The Bill of Rights lays down the law very clearly on the relationship of free speech to freedom of assembly. So in our view, if you want to improve a business, if it needs to change, then ideas are necessary and ideas are protected in 5/67 Thinking with No Blame.

A number of years ago we met with a California Union leader and he made an interesting observation: "If company employees were given "mutual respect" there would be no unions." Upon further explanation, he noted that to him respect was a two way street. Employees could really respect a boss and owner that listened to their ideas. And the boss and owner could really respect the employees when they proposed and implemented solutions to problems. It is this "mutual respect" that is key here. And it is hard to get going and sustain a positive work environment when there might have been animus in years past. And part of that "mutual respect" is the calm that is created with the "5/67 Thinking No Blame Game." When Management adopts the attitude that the company's employees are really its single most important resource and that management and staff are joined in seeking the best way to improve the business and create opportunities for everyone, then great things happen.

Lastly, as we have pointed out throughout this book, the 5/67 Thinking approach allows you to solve difficult and even Wicked Problems. However, this approach is most effective when the "No Blame Game" is actively supported and enacted by management. Otherwise, the critical element in making progress on difficult or Wicked Problems can be lost, which is incremental progress and learning. Specifically, the learning element will be attenuated or lost unless management celebrates progress and treats mistakes and mis-steps as lessons learned. 5/67 Thinking works because mistakes and mis-steps are made in small, incremental pieces of a project, not when taking on the entire problem all at once. Thus, 5/67 Thinking managers are able to create environments by applying the "No Blame Game" where team members thrive, mistakes have a minimum negative impact, and insights and learning are maximized. Teams get smarter and problems get solved quicker, and at a much lower cost than traditional 95/33 approaches.

We have all probably heard the maxim "Fail Forward". To turn failures into opportunities for future success, executives and leaders have to accept missteps as part of any project, and instead focus on the lessons learned and the new insights that will permit future success. Blaming team members for mistakes when attacking difficult and Wicked Problems will only lead to a culture wherein teams don't try anything that isn't already standard organizational policy or procedure.

This kind of cultural toxicity virtually assures innovation and problem solving will be minimized.

We would like to leave you with a quote from East of Eden, by John Steinbeck. He says:

> "...And this I believe: that the free,
> exploring mind of the individual human
> is the most valuable thing in the world.

And this I would fight for: the freedom of the mind to take any direction it wishes, undirected...And this I must fight against: any idea, religion, or government *or corporation* (the authors words) which limits or destroys the individual. This is what I am and what I am about."

John Steinbeck

East of Eden [3]

---

3 Steinbeck, John *East of Eden* Penguin Books, 1986 p. 171

CHAPTER 13

Pioneers & Settlers: Blending The Perfect Team

The term "Pioneers and Settlers" came from our years of working with War on Waste teams. Part of 5/67 Thinking is taking the simplest, most direct, low cost, and efficient solution to a problem, or a significant step towards solving a complex problem. An efficient team that works well together is an important part of 5/67 Thinking.

We've found that teams are made of two kinds of people, Pioneers, and Settlers. Pioneers are the ones who speak first, need to be heard, instinctively lead (or want to lead anyway). Settlers are the ones who listen, analyze, consider, and only then comment. Settlers also tend to be the ones who get the most actual work done. Thus defined, we have learned that teams of no more than two Pioneers and any number of Settlers (more than 2) tend to be the highest performing teams. The Pioneers keep things moving, keep the meetings short, and always push to take action. The Settlers nicely counterbalance the one or two Pioneers' natural aggressiveness.

As to how we determine who is a pioneer and who is a settler - it isn't very scientific. There are some people who are pioneers and some who are settlers, in the sense that some people are naturally outspoken and exhibit leadership qualities while other people naturally are work and outcome focused and get a lot done. We like to think that the whole human population breaks down into this binary division. We need both. And we can't all be pioneers, nor all settlers. In fact, we like the idea that there is some distribution of people into the two categories. And here is why.

The pioneers are the people with the wild ideas. They are the ones who push the limits of managers. In the Wild, Wild West, they were the guys who dared to go where no man had gone before. They set up the new territories and the settlers made the lands livable. There would have been neither development without the pioneers nor stability without the settlers.

The Pioneer is the entrepreneur who ventures out into the unknown. He is the adventurer who is looking for new territory, the entrepreneur making new markets. The Pioneer is the first to volunteer for the highly risky new assignment and the pioneer is very difficult to manage.

The Settler goes in after the pioneer and makes things work. The Settler stabilizes the rules of the business. The Settler is "steady as she goes." Settlers get things done.

But no organization can run with just Pioneers or Settlers.

A funny story about how this perceived distribution of personnel plays out in a company occurred a number of years ago. A CEO had noticed that one of his teams was not working as well as another one. When we asked him to tell us what the makeup of pioneers and settlers was, he almost started laughing. As soon as the question was asked, he knew what was coming next. In his situation, he had put 5 pioneers on the unsuccessful team. After the question was asked, the CEO immediately knew what to do. He replaced three of the pioneers with settlers and the team then was able to function. So the message here is don't put teams together with all pioneers or all settlers. Mix them up. By the way, there is a way to get 2 or 3 pioneers to work successfully together. However, that is another story entirely.

When it comes to determining whether a particular person is a pioneer or settler, it isn't very scientific. We don't have any particular test; we just use a "gut" feeling to guide the decision. In fact, when making assessments of people, don't worry that you might make a mistake in your assessment. There is nothing good or bad about either behavior. The classification is just a useful assessment tool to try to understand your management team and employees.

An interesting situation occurred at one company where we had explained the concept of Pioneers and Settlers to the management team. One of the executives who we had identified as a settler, really wanted to be pegged as a pioneer. He was obsessed with being a pioneer. He was the Vice President of Sales and was very good. He had an expectation that you have to be a pioneer to be a good salesman. But that isn't necessarily so. This guy was an excellent salesman. In his industry, a good settler was able to sell to the customers because they liked his laid back style. And his clients knew they could trust him and he would always follow up as expected. He had a good sense of humor that was very subtle. But he was a settler. There was nothing we could do about that. He had to live with it. Eventually, he did.

This section on Pioneers and Settlers was included to help managers look at their teams and have some experienced suggestions about how the teams are working or not working. Trust us, this is very helpful guidance as you manage problem solving teams. It provides a lens to help you filter the input that is hitting you as you try to manage your various projects. If teams are successful and making progress, you don't bother much with them. It is the teams that are struggling that this lens will help. Use it wisely.

CHAPTER 14

5/67 Thinking is a Non-linear Process

Traditional school programs teach us using linear methodologies. Linear thinking teaches us that every problem (the manifestation of an effect) has a unique cause. With linear thinking we are taught how to link a cause to an effect. It teaches that for each problem there is a "right solution". Further, it teaches that there is a right way to solve a problem. And the solution techniques are based on Aristotelian logic that has permeated Western thinking since the Middle Ages.

For example, accounting is a linear thinking discipline: capture data on a general ledger account, roll the numbers up to a summary account and make a decision based on the output. If the number is high, we do X, if it is right on we do nothing, and if it is low we do Y. Nice and ducky! Finance tells us what investment to make based on numbers but is less precise. Economics and finance tells us to open a new plant in Texas based on forecasts of economic indicators of a rapid growth in a particular segment of the market for the South Central section of the US. Whereas, the business of accounting is precise, the conclusions of finance are not always so. They differ from accounting by following what we call the logic of "Non-linear thinking." For example, the decision to put the plant in the South Central Section of the United States, had many competitive alternatives that might have been just as good in the long run. But a decision had to be made based upon the many competitive alternatives and the South Central option was chosen.

Unfortunately business decisions are largely like that. They are non-linear. They flow from intuition and not logic. Analytic tools are used to help fine tune the recommendation but they are never conclusive. They require jumps of thought and are probably more emotionally than rationally based. They amount to being the 5% solutions that we have discussed. Non-linear thinking says that there is more than one solution to any problem. Non-linear thinking says that there is no right way to solve a business problem.

In fact, we use the example of solving an equation in algebra to make an analogy here. If you are given 10 equations and 10 unknowns, you can solve the equations exactly following the linear thinking model of Algebra. But when you have 10 equations and 20 unknowns, many solutions will fit the equations. And that is what non-linear thinkers have to do. They choose one of the many solutions to those equations and run with it. Experience, intuition, logic, common sense, whatever you can muster is used to guide the recommendation or to make a decision.

We tell clients that it doesn't make sense to worry about whether you have the right solution because tomorrow's problem was today's solution. In other words, you make a decision today based on all the facts that you have at your fingertips and you run with the solution. Don't look back because you can be guaranteed that it is going to be a problem. "Today's solution is tomorrow's problem." This is important in 5/67 Thinking. It is "Failing Forward".

5/67 Thinking does not generate precise solutions. It gives employees who are implementing solutions lots of "wiggle room" in their implementation. We say in 5/67 Thinking, "that's OK if it doesn't work, find out why it didn't work, test another solution and move on." Just do it. But it works because it moves the company forward. It causes productivity to improve and people involved in the process become more engaged in the business because they were part of the solution.

5/67 Thinking says that it is better to do something than nothing. Action is more important than the immediate results. 5/67 Thinking says that progress is made when an action takes place. In both simple and difficult problems, that action and its attendant result has minor consequence if you are wrong. Just learn from your efforts and move on. However, in Wicked Problems you cannot jump into the problem with both feet lest you do more damage than good. As noted in Chapter 10, Wicked

Problems require a little more forethought with data captured to cast more light onto the problem to guide an incremental first step. In this case, anything is not better than nothing. We want carefully prepared action.

We usually don't do things to commit suicide in business. But we know that we will make mistakes. If it doesn't work that's OK because, like Edison, we have just learned another way that didn't work. That works with simple and difficult problems. In Wicked Problems, care is involved in making sure that you have enough information to make that first step. It is the best that 5/67 Thinking can deliver.

The War on Waste is rooted in non-linear logic. We don't need to blame someone to move forward. It doesn't make sense to blame someone for a problem. Just fix it. This is all part of creating a company with a sense of urgency. Make a decision, learn from it and then improve it.

The reason that the War on Waste works so well is that it has a singular focus. Eliminate this waste by following 5/67 Thinking. An alternative problem solving approach might begin by collecting data that quantifies the size of the waste. The "linear thinking" approach to this is to collect a bunch of data, and you can't do any analysis until you have a lot of it (statistically significant samples). And then you analyze the detail out of the data and it confuses the people that need to use the information. However, the "non-linear" approach would begin by collecting data for a few days (a little data - 5%) - spot check and see what that tells you. This is where we discovered the value of "5/67 Thinking." We looked at only 5% of the total data and we made a decision that was pretty solid when we looked back on the results.

We love to do this with the "anal-retentive" linear thinkers because it blows their minds. They can't make a decision unless there is tons of data to substantiate a point. We collect 5% of the needed data and make a decision. Go figure.

Let me repeat the problem that we discussed in Chapter 6 - Speed Analysis. This example said that instead of trying to analyze 20% of the years invoices or 6000 invoice which would have taken 4 weeks. They did a smaller sample (one week of data) that took them just 2 hours of class time to do the analysis. After they did that, remember that they didn't have "statistically significant" volumes of data but this analysis told them where they should spend their time to fix the problem.

The focus was on the process of one of the departments. I asked the CEO to give me his assessment of the problem before they started. He told me that his hunch was going to be that same department. And the fun thing about this process was that it only took the team of 5 people to analyze the data and come back with numbers in two hours that confirmed his guess.

The point here is that the 5/67 Thinking has its roots in non-linear thinking. But the focus on waste elimination keeps the team's problem solving on track. Eliminate the waste by collecting enough data to convince any decision making doubters that there is a problem and then you can go forward with your solution. If every decision in business followed this methodology, fewer catastrophic decisions would be made.

Many CEOs make decisions thinking that they have "statistically significant" numbers to back up their decision. Our point is that when all is said and done, most CEO's don't need a lot of data and information to guide their decision-making, they just need a little information, the 5%, and they will be right most of the time.

This is more of the rationale as to why the 5/67 Rule works. We had an early business mentor that told us that if 50% of his decisions turned out to be right, he was a genius. He felt that, as CEO, if he was close to 50% right in his decisions, the Board should allow him to keep his job.

CHAPTER 15

5/67 Take Aways: Better Projects, Better Decisions

5/67 Thinking boils down to a few key concepts. This chapter is really just an addendum for the super-busy executive who doesn't think they have the time to read this whole book, or doesn't fly often enough to read 80 pages before landing!

- Stupid problems can be solved directly

- Difficult problems should be decomposed and solved iteratively

- Wicked Problems should be analyzed and measured carefully. Do not rush to decompose and start! Be careful to not make the problem worse!

- Getting started is more important than planning the entire project.

- Being wrong doesn't hurt if you apply 5/67 Thinking. It helps. Really.

- Allow your teams to learn, make progress, and apply their newly acquired expertise to the next phase of the project. This provides a way to attack difficult problems without busting the budget and wasting time and money.

- The "No Blame Game" is a way to get your teams involved and freely expressing ideas. The 5/67 Tools keep people thinking about what really matters. Blaming someone who did something wrong in the past does NOT matter.

- Clarity of Roles and Clarity of Goals are longstanding hallmarks of well-managed teams, and 5/67 supports those maxims entirely. Best of all, 5/67 Thinking is fun. Using 5/67 Thinking is like solving a puzzle where you know a good solution can be found if you just try hard enough.

Last, but not least, feel free to reach out to the authors regarding your particular 5/67 problem. We're happy to exchange ideas and help you achieve your own success.

5/67 Problem Solving